PERFORMING TO THE MAX!

COPYRIGHT

Copyright © 2015
Copyright, Cox & Cox Consultants, Inc.
All rights reserved.
Published by Catsworth Press.

ISBN: 978-0-9861847-0-3

No part of this book may be reproduced or transmitted in any form by any electronic or mechanical means (including photocopying, recording, or information storage and retrieval) without permission in writing from the publisher (Catsworth Press) or by Cox & Cox Consultants, Inc.

The painting on the cover of this book is an original painted by the author and is available in reproduction or original customized artwork, painted on canvas ready for framing.

The following images courtesy of Shutterstock Inc.: Trumpet on musical notes as background close up/©Dusan Zidar; music charts with glasses and pen on top/©keko64; Detail of trumpet closeup/©Furtseff; Piano keys/©Tomislav Pinter, Musical notes and trumpet on wooden table/©Africa Studio.

CATSWORTH PRESS
822 King Street #114, Alexandria, VA, 22314
www.catsworth.com

PERFORMING TO THE MAX!

Richard H. Cox, MD, PhD, DMin

CATSWORTH PRESS
www.catsworth.com

DISCLAIMER

This book is not intended to diagnose or treat any physical or mental condition, and must not take the place of professional services. Any attempt to utilize the writing as such is specifically disallowed.

Cox & Cox Consultants, Inc.
Copyright 2015, All Rights Reserved.
1880 Brookwood Ave., Apt. 21
Burlington, NC 27215
Email: r-bcox@ix.netcom.com
Youtube: youtube.com/drrichardcox

TABLE OF CONTENTS

DEDICATION....................................	VII
PREFACE.......................................	IX
INTRODUCTION	13
LESSON ONE: **KNOW YOURSELF**	19
LESSON TWO: **KNOW YOUR INSTRUMENT**......................	29
LESSON THREE: **KNOW THE RULES**	35
LESSON FOUR: **KNOW THE MUSIC**	43
LESSON FIVE: **KNOW THE RESOURCES**........................	49
LESSON SIX: **KNOW THE AUDIENCE**..........................	55
LESSON SEVEN: **KNOW THE FIELD**	61
SUGGESTED READING..........................	65
PRAISE FOR PERFORMING TO THE MAX!	67
ABOUT THE AUTHOR	69

DEDICATION

This small, humble book is dedicated to the National Trumpet Competition, and especially to Dr. Dennis Edelbrock, its founder and Executive Director who introduced me to it, and to Dr. James Elswick who introduced me to Dr. Edelbrock and to NTC. It was Jim and Dennis who inspired me to become more deeply involved in working with student and professional musicians who face challenges that hinder them from performing to the max. It was my delight to be invited to join them in their rewarding efforts, and to continue for these eighteen years. May NTC have many more years of encouraging and supporting young trumpeters!

PREFACE

> "Canned music is like
> audible wallpaper."
>
> – Alastair Cooke (1908-)

Many players and performers reach an admirable level of professional expertise; however, few attain their maximum capabilities. We must encourage the development of fine musicians, lest all of the entertainment world turn to recorded music! Most of us really don't even know what our maximum potential might be. The reasons for this are many, but for the most part it is because we are not able, or have do not have the opportunity, to put the "whole picture together". For instance some of us play well but are not able to handle auditions, or we play very well but suffer stage fright, or we play well but are unable to attain sufficient self-discipline to maintain our own mental and physical health due to habits, addictions, and personality problems.

This little book is offered with the hope that more aspiring performers will put the whole picture together, and meet our nagging, sometimes less forgiving, problems head-on. It is possible for all of us to come closer to achieving our maximum potential when carefully evaluating ourselves in the light of the material in this book. I do not write as one who has achieved the maximum of my potential, or even close to it; but rather, as one who after eighty years of study and life has come to understand much more than I did as a young man. I am grateful for having had the privilege to study with some of the greatest teachers of my day, both in music and in my other pursuits of medicine, psychology and theology. I started on trumpet and piano at around age eight, and apprenticed with a wonderful violin maker when I was ten years of age. My teachers were wise, and the violinmaker especially started me on a journey early in life with his wisdom and experience. My only regret is that I did not pay enough attention!

Becoming a musician is so much more than learning to play an instrument. As a matter of fact, the musician is really the instrument and the musical instrument is simply the amplification of that person's ability and personality.

If this writing helps some to pay more attention, appreciate their teachers more, carefully look at their own potential, and establish goals as to how to get there, I will be sufficiently rewarded.

Richard H. Cox
Burlington, NC
2015

PREFACE

INTRODUCTION

> "After silence that which comes the closest to expressing the inexpressible is music."
>
> – Aldous Huxley (1894-1963)

Anyone who is a performer knows what it is to perform well. Every performer wants to perform to the absolute maximum of his/her ability! Furthermore, we know whether we have done our best or have settled for mediocrity. It is easy to become satisfied with less than the best when we are given false accolades or accept applause and praise when we know we have not put forth our best effort.

This does not mean that we should embrace a false humility. We all know of performers, who regardless of how well they have done, will minimize praise given to them after a concert, by saying, "thank you but I did not do all that well". It is okay to accept their thanks and appreciation because they have heard it through their appreciative ears, rather than through our critical musical analysis. We should thank them and be gracious to them – and save our self-criticism for our own practice room and to talk over with our teacher.

Doing your best, means exactly that -YOUR best. It means that you have matched and met your own expectations and have reached the bar that you have set for yourself during your own preparation. There are persons who somehow do better in rehearsal then they do in performance, and others seem to do better in performance than in rehearsal. I light up when I see the whites of their eyes! The notes that were black marks on white paper all of the sudden are images in my brain and my emotions project those memorized passages with feeling that is not present in the practice room. The reasons some do better in practice than in performance, and vice-versa are often unknown.

Sometimes it is stage fright, yet at other times it is not having the emotion of the music in the heart – black notes from white pages are sounds without meaning – without our emotions behind them. For many, like myself, doing our best sometimes comes out of us when we see the audience in front of us, particularly family members, friends, and teachers. Somehow we come to life and meet our expectations when they are accompanied by the expectations of others.

There are of course, performers who become overly anxious and even fall apart when facing an audience. The reasons for this are many and varied, but frequently have to do with being afraid that we will not meet their perceived expectations, which are unrealistic or imaginary on our part. I say, 'perceived', because we can only guess what an audience is expecting. Sometimes the handicapped playing comes from internalized problems that are too extensive to be discussed here. There are other fine books, including "Conquer Stage Fright" and "Managing Your Head and Body so You Can Become a Good Musician" (both by the author of this book), that may be helpful.

INTRODUCTION

Doing our best, becomes a matter of looking inside our self and trying to know what our "best" would be. Nothing takes the place of introspection, and willingness to meet our own internal expectations.

Performing is the art of leading others toward a well-planned goal. Simply looking on performing as an active entertainment is not sufficient. To perform is to accomplish, to complete, or to produce. Whether one is giving a public talk, playing a musical instrument, or performing a ballet maneuver, the goal is the same. That goal is to lead the audience toward more than the physical, visual, or auditory stimuli. It is to help the audience to move into a world that they did not inhabit when they sat down in that audience. Their ears, eyes, and brain should be engaged in an activity that steals them away from the things they were doing and thinking about before they sat down. Each performer will decide what that unique and individual world they will lead their hearers into. It may be a world of tranquility, excitement, or even sadness. Once this goal has been established the performer will be able to decide on the words, the music, the mood, the style of playing, the dynamics of the piece, and indeed, the "message" they wish to project through their instrument. Then, and only then, can we assist and lead the audience toward reaching that goal.

By carefully considering the five chapters in this little book, it is my hope that a performer will be assisted in performing at a higher level. Whether you are a beginner, and amateur or a well seasoned professional will make no difference. We never arrive at state where we do not reach for a higher goal or try to do better. The finest musicians, public speakers, and athletes all continue to practice diligently, not only in the technicalities of their specific instrument, voice, or bodily function, but in their mental attitude, personal introspection, and expectations of their audience.

It is suggested that the reader of this book utilize one chapter per week for a period of seven weeks. Give careful insight, honest self-criticism, conscientious recognition of both abilities and shortcomings, and an earnest desire to improve. At the end of each week a short period of reflection will be helpful. Making a few notes in a personal diary, writing in the front page of one of your favorite books, or even posting it on your study wall will help to imprint on your mind what you have learned that week. Habits are not made with one attempt – it is repetition – doing the *right* thing over and over – develops a pathway toward reaching our potential.

At the end of seven weeks, a longer session of personal reflection is recommended. An analysis of the seven weeks then should be made and summarized. Following this summarization, specific goals should be outlined with specific ideas for improvement. It is also most helpful if this list can then be taken to a mentor, teacher, or accomplished peer for additional help in implementation. Do not be embarrassed. The wise teacher or mentor will praise you for your diligence and sincerity. They lead you to a higher ground, and many in their own heart will be saying, "I wish I had done this exercise myself years ago!"

LESSON ONE: KNOW YOURSELF

"Observe all men; thy self most."

– Benjamin Franklin (1706-1790)

Nothing in the world takes the place of self-knowledge. The problem is that most of us only want to know the good about ourselves. Self-knowledge means exactly that, i.e., knowing as much as we can about ourselves, both the good, the bad, and the ugly - and that which we can improve. This knowledge is sometimes called "insight", which literally means "knowledge from inside". Yes, it is "you talking to you". It is as if we have a mirror reflecting our heart and soul into our eyes, ears, and brains. Plato is quoted as having said about 400 years before Christ , "know thyself ". He is also quoted as having said, "Wise men speak because they have something to say; Fools speak because they have to say something". Knowing oneself helps us to recognize which kind of person we are. We could apply this great saying to, "Some musicians play because they have a message to give; some play because they must play something". Even when we don't choose the music, we can look for the message and play it out!

The question becomes how do we know ourselves? Each person must travel his or her own journey in this regard. There are more ways to get to know oneself than could be discussed in a small volume like this. However, some of the following suggestions may be of help in getting started, and each method mentioned will no doubt open the door for other ways that you will discover all by yourself.

Of prime importance is time alone. In the busy, hectic and highly over stimulated world in which we live, it is essential to find time to be by our self. But we must work at making it happen. Our over-stimulated environment tends to transport us into other worlds all of the time. It is okay to visit other worlds – but we must also become intimately acquainted with our own. Simple quietude, meditation time, prayer time, and planned opportunity for self reflection must begin before any form of self-knowledge can result.

It is then necessary to be brutally honest with our self. Brutal honesty is not being brutal to our self but rather brutal to the un-truths, half-truths, and right-out lies that we let ourselves believe about our selves. We must allow honesty to be 100% and not permit us to gloss over areas that would be uncomfortable to recognize. We all have areas in our thinking, acting, and personality that we would rather ignore. But maturity does not come from that which we ignore but from that which we recognize and constantly strive to improve.

Improvement does not only come from what we see in our selves, but from many external sources as well. For instance, listening to our friends, parents, and teachers can be very helpful. Sometimes we think that if we listen to others it will get us off track, and that can happen. However; we can be discriminating, listen very carefully, thoughtfully, and respectfully, and at the same time select the information that we believe is useful. Outside sources are not always objective, but tend to be more objective than we are toward ourselves. Furthermore, sometimes what others tell us may seem terribly incorrect until we go back into our silent time and think about it very deeply. Never reject what others say at first thought, particularly those who have experience and the years of wisdom on their side. We can grow from what others tell us, even when they are mistaken.

It is important to look very specifically at what we like and do not like. Again, it is important to be honest in this endeavor. Particularly this is true during adolescence and young adulthood when we are prone to "think" that we like something, that is in truth simply a fad, or seems to be what other people like. The same is true for those things that we *think* we dislike. If thought about deeply we probably like things that others do not, and probably do not like many things that others do; but fool ourselves for the sake of "friendship" or being "cool". Knowing our self is to know the difference.

Knowing our self is also the ability to say "yes" and "no". Much of the time we are led to believe that we know ourselves best when we can say "no". Although at times that is true, but when we truly know ourselves we know what we can say "yes" to and what we can say "no" to. We do not put ourselves down by constantly saying "no", when our inner confidence tells us that we could say "yes". Neither do we say "yes" to something to that which our inner conscience tells us that we should say "no". The willingness to stand up for what we believe is a mark of maturity. Knowing our own values and abilities, rather than our need to be simply accepted by the crowd should be our goal.

A further mark of knowing our self is recognizing how to set reasonable yet challenging goals. Sometimes younger performers berate themselves because they have set goals that within any reason cannot be accomplished without many years of experience. Sometimes, without intending to do so, teachers and mentors are at fault in this regard. Rather than to set individual goals that are uniquely achievable by a student, they can set group goals which only some of the members of that group will achieve. This means that some fail and some succeed, rather than all members of the group succeeding, but only to the level of their ability. Knowing our self is incredibly important at this juncture so that we do not fall into the trap of allowing ourselves to be judged by the gifted, or those who fail, since most of us, most of the time, fall someplace in between.

Then, there are the physiological matters to which we must pay attention. Diet; knowing the foods that agree with us, which ones cause indigestion, which ones upset our system, etc. There are far too many dietary issues to discuss adequately here; however a few illustrations will start the interested student at looking at themselves. We need to recognize the foods that make performance difficult, such as too much caffeine, dairy products that produce too thick mucous, and too spicy foods that dull the sensations in the tongue. The singer may learn the lesson regarding drinking milk before singing, the hard way. The brass player may learn the hard way why after eating very spicy foods that tonguing "feels funny". A performer may wonder where the jittery nerves come from only to discover that they go away when they cut down on caffeine intake.

Medicines, both those prescribed by your doctor and those purchased over-the-counter need a careful look-see. For instance, many medications that seem "simple", are in fact very complex and produce many results not easily known at first. Aspirin for instance, may seem harmless, but can have serious side effects for some persons. Many products sold as "cold" or "allergy" medicines contain anti-histamine which can dry out the nose and mouth making it difficult to sing or play an instrument. Your doctor and dentist need to know up-front that you are a musician and you must help them to know best how to prescribe for you so that it doesn't interfere with your performance.

Knowing one's bodily schedule is also important. Some people are more naturally "day" people and others are more "night" people. We do know that sleep before mid-night is very important, and that sleep deprivation causes illness, chronic fatigue, dullness in thinking, and slower reflex response time. Pay attention to getting enough sleep – 7-8 hours for most people.

Everyone has some degree of spirituality, even those who say they are not "religious". They may not call it that, but we all have values, standards, and core beliefs. These affect our view of life, our attention to the "message" in music, and our relationships. We build much of our self-esteem on what others think of us; therefore, having friends that share our values is very important. Having a belief system that helps keep us on the "right road" will help us avoid many of the pitfalls that caused some professionals to fail when they could have succeeded.

Lastly, plan to be surprised by yourself. Regardless of how old you are, or how accomplished you become, or how well you think you know yourself, there will be surprises. You will do things that you thought you would never do, and fail to do other things that you were sure you would do. We constantly change, and our very person changes as well. That is called maturity and living life. Expect to grow, and in growth there are always rewards and disappointments. The winner is the one who can turn disappointments into opportunities. The one who wallows in unhappiness eventually becomes an unhappy person from the inside out and is miserable to be around. Expect to make mistakes and turn them into successes. Always look for the bright side and refuse to let your future be ruined by temporary set-backs. Life is full of beauty for those who have eyes to see it. But as Shakespeare said, "all to the jaundiced eye is yellow" – i.e., if we constantly look at things in a jaded way, soon everything looks jaded – even that which is not.

Here are some helpful hints: it is very helpful for one to put into writing a personal oath. Think this through slowly, carefully, and honestly and do not do it frivolously. This is your promise to yourself! Don't write it in blood, but you might consider putting it in ink so that it cannot be erased and changed if you become "weary in well doing"!

As ridiculous as it may sound, writing down what you believe, your goals, how you expect to attain them, the resources upon which you are going to lean, and a reasonable timeline is very helpful. Further, and perhaps even more ridiculous is the suggestion that after you have written your oath, that you read it over to your self regularly, perhaps even every day. Then to be even more helpful, at the risk of being even more ridiculous, it is unbelievably helpful to read your oath to yourself while looking in a mirror. In literature, this kind of behavior is called a soliloquy, which literally means, talking to yourself!

LESSON ONE: KNOW YOURSELF

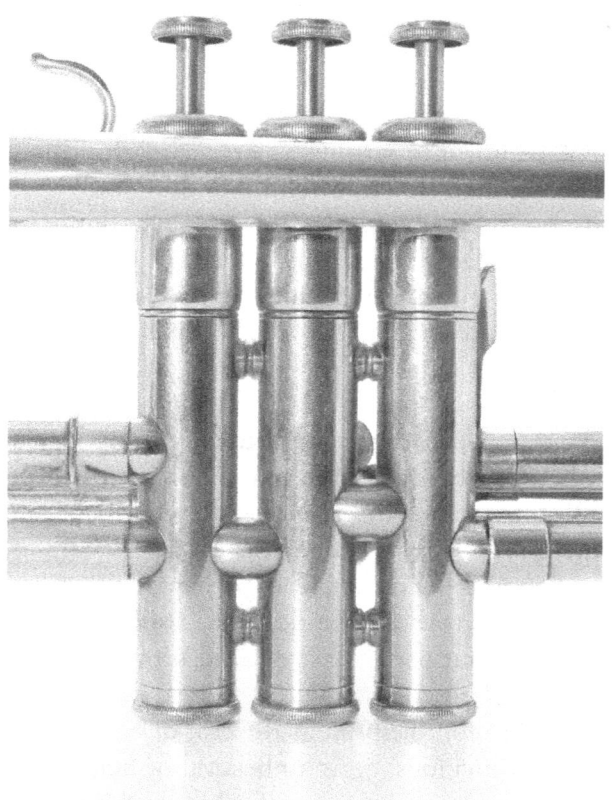

LESSON TWO:
KNOW YOUR INSTRUMENT

> "A musician may suddenly reach a point at which pleasure in the technique of the art entirely falls away, and in some moment of inspiration, he becomes the instrument through which music is played."
>
> – *Edwin Diller Starbuck (1866-1947)*

No two instruments are alike whether you're speaking of trumpets, violins, or the human voice. Two trumpets of the same make, made on the same day, plated with the same material, and marketed as "the same", are not. Although indistinguishable to a non-musicians ear, their tone will not be the same, their mechanism of action will differ, and a well seasoned trumpet player will know the difference. Those who play violins and other stringed instruments know altogether

LESSON TWO: KNOW YOUR INSTRUMENT

too well the difference in any two instruments. The wood from which they are made, the kind and amount of varnish that is used to finish it, the humidity and other environmental conditions in which it was seasoned, and many other factors all make a difference.

It is totally unnecessary, since we all know it so well, to discuss differences in the human voice. Most people know us by our voice over the telephone or when speaking to them before they see us. The human voice is so uniquely recognized that this manuscript is being typed by a computer that has no ability to see the writer; a voice-recognition program. Trumpet players will know their own instrument even with their eyes closed. Many famous pianists travel with their own piano. The tone of their own piano is deeply ingrained in their mind, and the unique touch of the keyboard and action of the pedals is an integral part of their professional performance.

Understanding our instrument is critical to maximizing our performance. Each instrument has its own idiosyncrasies, and each person's playing has learned to adapt to these unique differences. For instance, valves on different trumpets function differently. Some are smoother than others, some are faster than others, some are prone to stick, while some are rotary valves and others are piston valves. Spending time with the unique differences of the instrument we are going to use for performance is critical. The instrument is an extension of the performer and should be as well known to the performer as are her or his hands, fingers, birth date, or home address.

We do not always know "why" an instrument is different. But we know it is. We have come to recognize a distinctly individualized sound. We may not know, and in truth, do not need to know, the "why" for these differences. The technician, the instrument designer, the craftsman, or the metallurgist may tell us the "why", if we really need or want to know. However: if we ask a performer what is different about their instrument, they are apt to say "I don't know, but it just feels different", or they may say "it just doesn't sound like my own", or they may simply say it doesn't fit me", or more idiosyncratic statements like, "I can't get around on it".

When we get to really know our instrument is when we can forget it and let it be an extension

LESSON TWO: KNOW YOUR INSTRUMENT

of our own personality. After all, a trumpet for instance, is nothing more than a megaphone through which we blow air and amplify the notes we make. It is the musician behind the megaphone that makes the difference. Technique does not make music, it makes carefully produced sounds. Knowing our instrument intimately is critically so that we can take care of it and forget it.

Knowing our instrument allows us to choose the instrument that matches a particular kind of performance or piece of music. While this is not true of instrumentalists who rely only upon one instrument, it is particularly true of trumpet players who have an option between instruments in different keys and with different tonal qualities. This is a rare advantage since it occurs with few if any other instruments.

Sometimes, particularly the seasoned musician, will assume that instruments are like some brands of clothing in which "one size fits all". As a result, many players are handicapped by not knowing or having the opportunity or encouragement to play an instrument that fits their physiology the best. Professional musicians will often have minor changes made on their instrument to fit their own anatomical peculiarities. For instance, a trumpet may need a thumb trigger rather than a thumb-saddle to fit their particular hand. Many saxophone players are handicapped by attempting to play a saxophone which requires a greater degree of finger-stretch than they possess. Admittedly, there are fewer adjustments that may be made to most stringed instruments, including the piano. Since the voice is also considered an instrument, all voice teachers know the importance of singing within one's range thus maximizing their musical talent. The woodwind player will know the unique needs and characteristics of their instruments, as will the string players, and percussionists. No detail is too small. After all, someone has rightly said, "the devil is in the detail" – so are the angels!

Understanding and getting to know our instrument takes time. The story is told, whether or not it is true is not known, but it is said that the great trumpet player, Raphael Mendez kept his trumpet with him virtually 24 hours a day. It is also said that he even slept with it. Recognizing his incredible virtuosity makes this a believable story whether it is true or not. Learning the feel of the instrument, it's weight, its balance, the wide variety of musical colors that it can produce, the difference between how it sounds to the player and how it sounds to the audience, and learning the many other small but important unique features is essential for the player who wants to make the instrument an extension of the self.

LESSON THREE: KNOW THE RULES

"In a world of peace and love, music would be the universal language."

– David Thoreau (1870-1862)

There is much more to performing than knowing the music if you are a musician, or the script if you are a speaker. Excellent performers flub up all the time simply because they do not pay attention to the rules. Ask the questions, make sure you understand the answers, and make sure you understand what is expected. Part of performance is to know the rules, all the way from appearance to attending to the expected code of conduct.

There are rules regarding dress codes. This one issue has cost many musicians a gig, or even a career. Showing up with white sox, forgetting

LESSON THREE: KNOW THE RULES

the black bow-tie, or wearing brown shoes or sneakers with a tuxedo are all 'no-no's". Female performers who feel that they must test the limits of propriety with their attire can be embarrassing for them and in spite of being good musicians may cost them future jobs.

Not enough can be said about showing up on time. "On time" doesn't mean at the hour of performance. It means 30 to 45 minutes earlier – enough time to make sure everything is in place and that the contractor or band director does not have to pace the floor hoping that you will show up.

Personal hygiene must be high on the list. There is nothing worse than having those sitting next to you noticing body odor, poor personal grooming, and physical sloppiness. Your musical talents won't overcome the smells or the looks. Remember, we only have one chance to make a first impression!

Pay attention to your role, i.e., are you the one soloing or are you a supporting player. The second trumpet, for instance, must always try to match the principal's style as much as possible and not attempt to stand out or "steal the show". Your job is to make the soloist or principal look good. Play under but support, and be ready to play the unexpected when emergency calls.

When another player (or you) makes a mistake – regardless of how terrible it is – you do not make faces – and you don't stare at them!

Know when to bow and how to bow. Bowing is a mark of appreciation for the response of the audience, but also is a demonstration of the performer's appreciation of the audience. It must show gratitude and humility. It is not a time to gloat, however; neither is it a time to act as if it is unimportant and that you dismiss the appreciation of the audience. When playing in a group, bowing is done together and one must not appear to be "taking all the glory" and attempting to make the bow into a solo performance!

You always need to have pencil ready to make notes on the music - only a pencil, never a pen – so that you don't have to rely on memory for changes and dynamics the conductor wants.

Never practice another player's solo on stage – although you may want – and need- to be ready to play another player's part, it should be practiced in your own practice room. However; a wise player is ready to play another part if needed at the last minute.

Never cancel a gig for a better offer! Ethics demand that you be known as reliable, responsible, and that you keep your word and do not put another group in jeopardy because you bailed out. There may be unusual circumstances where you need to cancel – very, very rare- and must be handled professionally with all persons involved.

When there is an expected order for tuning up, you follow the routine – only in high school band do all instruments *try* to tune up at the same time (usually quite in disregard for the band director). Is that why they are often out of tune?

Musicians have failed due to some of the most ridiculous things that can be mentioned, such as forgetting their music, showing up with a trumpet and no mouthpiece, or needing a Harmon mute when all they brought was a straight one. I don't think I have ever heard of a violinist forgetting the bow, but I guess it probably has happened.

Having valve oil, slide lubricant, extra reeds, extra strings, and the other items that only the instrumentalist knows, must be kept in mind. A guitar player who has not arranged for amplification may be at a fatal loss.

A common oversight is not paying attention to common courtesy. Respect for the conductor – regardless of how demanding, ego-centric, and ridiculous- is an absolute must. Respect for fellow musicians – even when they make glaring mistakes – is required. Taking care not to dribble spit all over the floor from a brass instrument – particularly when in the chancel of a church or other carpeted settings where it is obviously out of order. Professionals do not treat concert halls and sanctuaries like high school students treat the gym!

In order to "play to the max", learning to pay attention to items such as these is critical early on in the performer's education. There are many more "rules" that are not mentioned here, furthermore, many rules apply specifically to each group and are understood for that group only. Knowing the rules makes the game a lot easier!

In my clinics and workshops over the years I have noticed a great decrease in the decorum and common courtesy among students, and I am sorry to say also among some professionals, at rehearsals and even performances. I have even noticed players talking, oiling their valves, or other distracting activity when a soloist is playing! High school students who want to get ahead are wise to get into the music room on time, have their instrument ready, and be sitting (not talking), looking over the music, or getting "their head in the right place" to play. Habits such as these stick with you later when jobs depend on them – and, so do the bad habits – that can cost you auditions and jobs.

Every group has its own unique rules and expectations. Going out of the road to learn them and taking extra care to observe them can pay big dividends. Many a student has forfeited a first-chair promotion, not due to poor playing of the instrument, but poor playing of the rules. There are many "small" items that may seem inconsequential, but in fact they make lasting impressions – good and bad.

For instance, sitting sloppy with your legs crossed while playing, emptying your water-key on another's players shoe, or talking to another player over the head or instrument of several others. Then there is the player that knocks over someone else's instrument after diving to the floor to retrieve their scattered music on the floor. Or the one who arrives late and has to climb over several other instruments and players to get to their seat – only to remember that they left your music someplace else and have to climb back over several to get out again- more, more, more – you know them all!

Life is full of rules – the sooner we understand and accept that, the better adjusted we can become. Music, of all things in the world is governed by rules of all sorts. The more that a young student understands the rules, the less problem he/she will be for the band director or concert-master. Here again, most rules you simply must know – often no one will take the time to teach you – they simply will not invite you to play and you may never know why. More

LESSON THREE: KNOW THE RULES

senior players should be encouraged to take the younger ones "under the wing" and let them in on the unspoken rules of a group. By the same token, the younger ones should not be shy about seeking out an older, more experienced peer to serve as a mentor.

It is true that we like to make our own rules, but in music it is always a team effort, and most of the time the rules are made for us, either by the composer or the conductor; however, the limitations of our instrument, our own abilities, our society, and the group in which we choose to play also add to the rules we must apply. Even concert soloists are plagued by the rules of other people and the audiences for whom they play. So, if you are young and just starting out – learn the rules – obey the rules – show respect for the rules – and let the rules bring you joy rather than frustration.

LESSON FOUR: KNOW THE MUSIC

> "The notes I handle no better than many pianists. But the pauses between the notes – ah, that is where the art resides!"
>
> *– Artur Schnabel (1882-1951)*

We can now turn to knowing the music. Music is not composed in a vacuum. It is composed by an individual, at a particular place, in a specific period of time, and intended to convey a special message. Not knowing these particulars would be like reciting the Gettysburg address without knowing who wrote it, for what purpose, and where it was first delivered. Asking an audience to enter into a message that you are to deliver, musically or otherwise, would be like inviting them to a party or function without telling them the date, the time, or where the event is to be held.

LESSON FOUR: KNOW THE MUSIC

We can look at the message of the music even more deeply by considering the dynamics. These are markings that can be looked upon like special instructions being required for a given event. One typically does not wear formal attire to a basketball game, or sportswear to a formal wedding. The often overlooked workings in a piece of music designate what that particular piece of music "is wearing", and how it's particular appearance is to be announced. Phrasing amounts to far more than the subtle marks on the page. It speaks to the expression of each note much as each word in a sentence has its own time and space within a paragraph, and that paragraph within the story. It is only when one understands the unique message of a given piece of music that "musical-license" can be taken. However, when that piece of music is clearly understood, there is a great deal of liberty available while maintaining the integrity of the time signature and written dynamics.

"Knowing" a piece of music essentially involves nearly, and much of the time actually, memorizing it. Until it is deeply embedded in the brain we are not able to fully appreciate its power. Until the music has moved the player, it is not apt to move those who hear it. By memorizing the music, the brain is able to then give it the performer's personality, and take the players mind off of the notes, the technique, and the instrument, and place it on the message. As long as the brain is hampered by the specifics of information, it is not able to relax itself and transport the performer's message in a transcendent fashion.

Knowing the music means to play it at different tempos, different styles, with different tone colors, and with different emphases, based upon one's knowledge of the composer, the purpose for which it was composed, and the audience to which it is being performed. A great deal of imagination is required at this point. Gaining expertise in this manner is often enhanced by practicing while being recorded and listening to it back. It is also very helpful to practice a piece of music, or give the speech, in the auditorium or room where he will be performed. This allows the performer to experience that piece of music within the acoustics and the ambience of that particular venue. A beautiful performance can be ruined by not paying attention to what it sounds like in the actual room where it is performed – it is always different than in the practice room.

Playing the notes is frequently not sufficient, to genuinely know a piece of music. If the music has lyrics, they should be studied carefully. The words will tell the performer what message the composer intended to give. Whether it is rejoicing, pathos, or some other emotion will become clear. Further, understanding the lyrics will frequently allow the performer to better understand both the key signature and the time signature better. There are many compositions, of course, that do not have lyrics. In that case it is important to understand where and why that piece of music was written and attempt to bring to life the reality of that particular musical message.

As important as playing notes obviously is, sometimes the rests and the pauses are equally important. The brain needs time to integrate what it has heard, and after a very brief period of assimilation it is ready and even curious as to what comes next. Performers who rush through pauses and do not pay attention to the fullness of a rest is like a speaker who rattles on incessantly without taking a breath.

Playing with expression comes from the heart. When playing with a group there is less opportunity for individual expression unless you are playing a solo, or principal player. Hopefully, if you are not the principal player, that person will be playing with a wonderful expression that you can support. Students should actively seek opportunities to play in as many different size groups as possible, and in small groups of all sorts in order to seek opportunities to solo, in order to develop different skills and styles of expression.

The great trumpet player Timofei Dokshizer said, "I only play the pieces that like me". What a wonderful concept! One suspects that he meant both the pieces that he instinctively could play well and that fit his personality, while rejecting those that did not project his message. This is truly, "knowing the music!"

LESSON FOUR: KNOW THE MUSIC

LESSON FIVE: KNOW THE RESOURCES

"Everywhere in the world, music enhances the hall, with one exception: Carnegie Hall enhances the music."

– Isaac Stern (1920-)

There are many resources available to help us with performing to the max. The wise young and old musician alike will look critically at the many resources available today. They do not all help- some hurt. Some things help one person and not another. A new mouthpiece that is the latest thing "since sliced bread" for one player may be the worst possible invention for another. There is virtually no end to the resources available for various instruments, and the following are only listed to encourage your mind into looking at what is available, and evaluating them in the most careful light:

LESSON FIVE: KNOW THE RESOURCES

Mouthpieces and other mouthpiece gimmicks. There are thousands of rim sizes, cup styles and depths, double cups, screw on rims, spring-loaded "no-pressure kinds, shapes from round to oval to cupped-out, silver plated, gold plated, raw brass (never good), stainless steel, plastic, wood, titanium, long-shank, short-shank, dozens of back-bores, and throat sizes, on, and on. Most of the time, the major correction for a poor performing mouthpiece is more practice! However; a quality teacher will lead the student into the correct mouthpiece with a great deal of deliberate and careful thought. Jumping from one mouthpiece to another without very careful attention is rarely, if ever, (probably never) recommended.

Of books, there is no end. Books are much like food; some are to be tasted, some to be chewed, and some to be swallowed. Only a few are in the latter category. Students sometimes hurt themselves by constantly switching from one school of thought to another. Many different styles and techniques have evolved over the years, and virtually all of them have produced great players – but they are not all the right one for any given person. The standard, tried and true method books are still the "bibles" and should be mastered first before experimenting with the more exotic approaches.

Study music literature as well as technique and method books. Read books on the history of music, biographies of great musicians, musical theory, and the stories of the great operas, the stories of great concerts, and seek advice and suggestions from veterans in the performance world. Do not only read the performance histories about musicians – performance is performance, and the thinking and habits of great performers, whether it be in golf, dance, or music, have many similarities. The thinking of a great baseball player or sky-diver might well help you to perform your music better!

Do not overlook the wonderful availability of CDs, videos, and recordings of great players. Also, do not reject recordings (even on vinyl or tape) just because they are old and "out of date". Many of the great artists are only to be found on those media. The difference between "good" playing and "great playing" is sometimes very small. You must listen for the tiny, sometimes almost imperceptible nuances in these

LESSON FIVE: KNOW THE RESOURCES

performances, such as the tone, the style, the technique, the dynamics, the way a piece starts – and ends -, the phrasing, the emotion behind various passages, the range of notes (not all great playing is in the stratosphere – and it is not all loud!), the color of the tone, the musical liberty taken with tempo, tonguing, (or bowing), the way the performer holds your interest, and much more.

Never pass up an opportunity to hear a performer in person. Live concerts excite the mind and imbed permanent impressions in your sub-conscious brain. You are never aware of all that you have learned, but it will show later. You learn much more than whether the music was played well or not. It is helpful to listen to the music from a recording, if possible, prior to the live performance.

The whole picture of player interaction, seating arrangements, amplification, dress, relationship to the conductor, staging, lighting, professional behavior, and much more is constantly being registered in your brain when you are there in person. Study the players, pay particular attention to everything from posture to the way a musician holds an instrument – let no detail slip by unnoticed. Remember, the difference between the musician that gets the job and the one who does not is frequently not their ability to play, but small things they will never be told.

Invest in resources – do not "spend" for anything. This difference is subtle but important. When you invest in something you expect a return – it will bear interest – it grows and becomes more than you put into it. When you spend, you receive goods that will soon be gone – it means exactly what it says – you "spent" (got rid) of it. Investing in musical accoutrements is serious business since there is no limit to the "things" that you can buy which do not necessarily promise a return to you. Don't jump on every new gadget that comes along- but do not, by the same token, ignore inventions that shorten the learning cycle and improve technique more quickly. Consult with your teacher and listen to the playing and the advice of the well-experienced players of your instrument.

There are many theories about teachers. Some believe that a student should stick with one teacher and listen to no body else's advice. This,

LESSON FIVE: KNOW THE RESOURCES

in my opinion, is too protective and smacks of professional jealousy. There are entirely too many "correct" methods, and far too much experience to be housed in one brain! On the other hand, switching from one teacher to another all the time is also most confusing. If you study the lives of the great performers, most of them had a few teachers and stuck with each of them for several years. Many have only two or three primarily teachers in a lifetime, and proudly state that they are the student of (fill in the name.) This is usually a tribute to both the teacher and the student.

Gaining tid-bits from clinics, workshops, and lectures is wonderful, and is not the same of switching teachers. There is nothing wrong with taking an occasional lesson from another teacher, either, particularly when you are more advanced. Great teachers teach more than how to play an instrument. As a matter of fact, it is probably not possible to teach "how to play". It is only possible to teach you how to teach yourself how to play. Great teachers teach how to become a respected human being with the qualities that transcend the music you play.

LESSON SIX: KNOW THE AUDIENCE

> "On stage, I make love to 25,000 different people, then I go home alone."
>
> – *Janis Joplin (1943-1970)*

Audiences are not all the same – even those that look alike. Most audiences are made up of an extremely wide range of IQ's, interests, abilities, likes and dislikes, and expectations. Some have come to a concert with great enthusiasm and may know the music as well as you, the performer. Others did not even want to attend and were nearly "dragged" along by a friend. Some will stay alert and watch your every move, notice your every note, and anticipate your next breath. Others will go to sleep – and hopefully not snore too loudly!

LESSON SIX: KNOW THE AUDIENCE

Always be respectful of the audience regardless of what they do. Especially when you are a paid performer, even the people who act inappropriately have usually paid to hear you. It sounds unfair – and it is- but who said it was always fair?

Try to know ahead of time as much as is possible about your audience. If it is a church in which you are performing, try to know the style of their worship. Is it more or is it less formal? Will you be playing facing the audience or are you playing from a balcony? Is the room "live" or is it heavily carpeted (which will change how you project your tone)? Will you be playing with congregational singing, with an organ, with a piano, or without accompaniment? The "audience" includes all that goes into making up the total environment to which you are playing. It is not uncommon, particularly at Easter sunrise services, to play out-of-doors – which presents an entirely different picture of environment and human participants – sometimes rain, cold, poor lighting, wind that blows the music, and instruments that are hard to keep in tune.

The audience of a group of high school students is likely to be very different from a group of parents, or a community concert. They may be talking and laughing while you are performing, and not talking about you or laughing at you at all- just being immature (and disrespectful) – and, although we deplore such behavior, we have no choice but to accept the world as it is and do our best to adapt to it.

The audience may be an audition committee. This presents a totally different picture – a highly competitive one, at that. When accepting this wonderful opportunity, wisdom will take the performer to a wise, experienced player who has been there before, for coaching, advice, and encouragement. Even when auditioning for a local musical group, or when hoping to "move up a chair", the same attention should be paid and start developing the habits that will serve you later in even more advanced situations.

Be gracious and friendly after the performance – when the opportunity is present, meet people in the audience, thank them for coming, accept the accolades and even the criticisms graciously.

LESSON SIX: KNOW THE AUDIENCE

It is often necessary to adapt to conditions or audience expectations that you cannot anticipate. Recently when performing in a very "live" room, a piece on which I had intended to play a C trumpet sounded very brash, edgy, and just too overpowering, plus I was playing to an audience of elderly persons, many of whom would have hearing aids. Changing to a more mellow toned Bb trumpet and adapting a softer playing style solved the problem. On another occasion, what was planned for a Bb trumpet just did not convey the message in a very bright room (hardwood floors, much glass, no carpeting, high and hard ceiling), so the flugel horn was substituted and worked well. A younger audience might have been okay with the brighter and more edgy tone, but hearing aids are not very forgiving of harsh sounds. Take into account the room, the audience, their unique needs (such as hearing aids), and adapt accordingly. A true professional is not like the old saying, "to a carpenter who has only a hammer, all problems are nails" – to the musician who has only one approach, every situation has the same answer. – Not good. We must be adaptable, willing to make changes without warning, and have lots of "tools" in our bag to pull out and use as we need them.

Sometimes the music we must play is not our favorite, but we must be able to put it into our heart and play it as if it were our most favorite piece in the whole world in order to bring it to life for others. It is actually possible to "lose yourself" when performing. I was recently called upon to play a solo and found the piano accompanist seemingly knowing only one key signature and time signature. There was no way she was going to follow me – and there was certainly no way I could follow her – so, what to do? The answer was to play without accompaniment. It turned out to be a total surprise in that midway through the piece, I literally forgot where I was or what I was playing – everyone remarked at how deeply emotionally they were touched. Sometimes, obstacles become blessings!

LESSON SIX: KNOW THE AUDIENCE

LESSON SEVEN: KNOW THE FIELD

> "Music was my way of keeping people from looking through and around me. I wanted the heavies to know I was around."
>
> – *Bruce Springsteen (1949-)*

Early in one's musical career it is important to survey the field, learn what the competition is, what are the opportunities, and what it takes to get to the place that you desire.

The vast majority of even good instrument players in high school and college do not continue once they graduate. This is tragic but true. It may well be that the opportunities were not evaluated carefully or at all. It is also often true that counting the cost to get to the top is just too high. The self-imposed discipline of daily practice, personal devotion to the field, and the sacrifices to get to the top is as great, and much greater, than for most any other profession. Few other professions require the individual time in a practice room that is required of instrumentalists to play an instrument well.

If a career as an instrumentalist is your goal, developing the habits of self-discipline, daily practice, and top academic performance is a necessity, before thinking about applying to a fine school of music. Then, and only then, study the schools – look at the entrance requirements and make sure you don't come up short when graduating from undergraduate studies. See what scholarships are available and the level of accomplishment necessary to be a serious contender. Think carefully whether you want to specialize in jazz, classical or other form of playing, or a combination – since different schools offer greater and lesser opportunities for different kinds of music. Know your mobility possibilities – can you make a geographical move – do you have the funds to move, rent housing, pay for transportation, living expenses, etc. Do you have the variety of trumpets (if you are a trumpet major) required, i.e., trumpet in C, B♭, Piccolo, and possibly one in D, and E♭, and maybe a flugel horn. All are not necessary, but make sure which ones are considered essential for the program you undertake. Look carefully at what kind of future life you may have if you make a given choice. Early decisions have increasingly important ramifications as you grow older and have greater responsibilities such as a family.

There are many opportunities to enjoy playing well at many levels other than principal in a major symphony. There are comparatively few positions available in symphony orchestras, and even fewer in paying symphonies, and fewer still in positions with symphonies that pay adequately to make it a full-time paying job so that other income is not necessary.

This should not be a deterrent to becoming "good". Teaching, public school, private school, colleges, universities, schools of music, the military, etc. are very rewarding and stable positions. In many cases such a position offers the "best of all worlds" in that one can play in a fine regional musical group, solo independently for additional income, teach privately if wishing to do so to supplement a steady income source, a pension

LESSON SEVEN: KNOW THE FIELD

plan for retirement, and often tuition benefits for family members who would wish to attend that particular academic institution. Quality teacher/players are very much valued and they should be looked upon as having responded to a very high calling.

Local bands, orchestras, and musical groups are also rewarding. This is particularly the case for the musician who wishes to be a "pro-am" person, i.e., amateur-professional. Many doctors, ministers, and other professional persons thoroughly enjoy a life of music "alongside" their professional work. There is a real need for good players to play in church orchestras, local community bands, local swing bands, quintets, and other musical groups.

Keep playing to the max and opportunities will arise and often even surprise you. Good luck and practice well!

> "A wise man will make more opportunities than he finds."
>
> *– Francis Bacon (1561-1626)*

SUGGESTED READING

Ayers, A. Jean, Sensory Integration and the Child. Los Angeles: Western Psychological Services, 1979

Campbell, Don G., Introduction to the Musical Brain, 2nd Edit.. MMB Music, St. Louis, 1992

Cox, Richard H., Issues of Life, InSync Press, Sanford, FL, 2001

Cox, Richard H., Managing Your Head and Body so You Can Become a Good Musician, 3d. edit., Colorado School of Professional Psychology Press, Colorado Springs, CO., 2006

Cox, Richard H., Conquer Stage Fright, Cox & Cox Consultants, Inc., Chapel Hill, NC 2009

Goode, Michael I., Stage Fright In Music and Its Relationship to the Unconscious, 2nd edit., Trumpetworks Press, Oak Park, IL 60301, 2003

SUGGESTED READING

Hickman, David, Trumpet Pedagogy, Hickman Music Edition, Chandler, AZ, 2006

Knoblauch, Steven H., The Musical Edge of Therapeutic Dialogue, The Analytic Press, Hillsdale, NJ, 2000

Levitin, Daniel J., This is Your Brain on Music, Plume, New York, 2006

Lewis-Lucinda, Broken Embouchures, Oscar's House Publishing, NJ., 2002

Schneiderman, Barbara, Confident Music Performance, MMB, St. Louis, 1991

PRAISE FOR PERFORMING TO THE MAX!

"Dr. Richard Cox, a renown expert in the arena of helping performers achieve excellence and optimum performance levels, consistently draws upon his vast knowledge of medicine, psychology and theology to elevate others. His writings and clinics inspire, and he practices what he preaches with his own trumpet performances! More than that, he is a deeply caring and benevolent individual, and I am proud to also call him a trusted friend and colleague."

Alan Hood
Professor of Trumpet
University of Denver

PRAISE FOR PERFORMING TO THE MAX

"Dr. Richard Cox is of the upmost authority on the subject of musical performance and stage fright. I have personally gained and witnessed with many collegues his expertise. I would highly recommend any of his books on the subject."

Ken Robinson
Founder and President of Robinsons Remedies
Former Trumpet with Maynard Ferguson and
Big Bop Noveau

"Dr. Richard Cox has graced us with his knowledgeable presence myriad times at UNC School of that Arts. He is an indefatigable resource on all things performance-related; his simple and practical steps for performance success reflect his excellent and noteworthy combination of degrees and long life experience as a physician and psychologist, topped off by his perspective as a trained pastor. His is a trustworthy voice!"

Judy Saxton
UNC School of the Arts, Eastern Music Festival
Trumpet Artist Faculty

ABOUT THE AUTHOR

Dr. Richard Cox writes from a depth of experience and professional training covering more than 60 years as a physician, psychologist and musician. His work has been endorsed by Adolph (Bud) Hirseth, Frank Kaderabek, Ronald Modell, Al Hood, Dennis Edelbrock, Michael Davison, David Hickman, Terry Warburton, Fred Powell, Judith Saxton, and many others. Dr. Cox has published extensively in these fields and has been a regular presenter at the National Trumpet Competition, International Trumpet Guild, Interlochen Center for the Arts, The American Academy of Pain Management, as well as psychological and medical conferences. He has performed, taught, and lectured nationally and internationally. He was recently written up in an American Psychological Association publication as "A skilled trumpeter, Dr. Richard Cox uses both his music and psychology expertise to help other musicians address stage fright and avoid injuries that can result from improper instrument positioning or overuse". He is known as the "go to" person for physical, psychological, and performance issues. Also, public speakers and other performers have found his work highly beneficial. He is currently faculty at Duke University Medical School; Affiliate Scholar, Georgetown University Medical Center's Pellegrino Center for Clinical Bioethics; and is listed as a Scholar at Oxford University (UK); and is a prolific artist, Conn-Selmer Musical Instruments. Contact Information: clinics, presentations, and writings.

Dr. Cox may be contacted at:
r-bcox@ix.netcom.com

Richard H. Cox, MD, PhD, DMin

www.ingramcontent.com/pod-product-compliance
Lightning Source LLC
Chambersburg PA
CBHW061509040426
42450CB00008B/1540